Conversation Books — Now you're talking!™

EVERYTHING YOU *NEVER* WANTED TO KNOW ABOUT SEX

Larry Balsamo & Sandra Bergeson

TDC Books ★ Chicago

Published by

TDC, Incorporated
1470 Norwood Avenue
Itasca, Illinois 60143

Copyright 1994, TDC Incorporated

Manufactured in the United States of America

"Conversation Books" is a registered trademark of TDC, Inc.

Cover design and illustrations by Antonio Roskolnokov, Copyright 1994 TDC, Inc

ISBN: 1-884057-10-1

First Printing - January 1995

To the residents of Blue Ball, Arizona and Beaver, Pennsylvania, may they someday come together in Lovelock, California.

Conversation Books

With the busy schedules of today's hectic world and the onset of the home entertainment center, people have all but lost the ability to communicate on a personal level. Parents find it next to impossible to congregate their family at a dinner table, let alone get them to talk to each other. When finally gathered, attempts at conversation tend to resemble a TV talk show, predictable questions and prefunctory answers spiced with just a pinch of bickering. The remote control has become everyone's favorite companion. Ask any marriage counselor.

Still, the human being is a social creature which yearns to be in relation to one's self and with others. We all have something to say. We've just forgotten how or when to say it.

The *Conversation Book* series has been specifically designed to stimulate the lively art of conversation. The information contained in each edition is meant to be shared with a group for open discussion.

Some of these books will make you laugh. Others may provoke heated arguments. But each will provide hours of insightful communication with whomever you choose to share the contents. They are, however, just books. If certain questions or statements hit too close to home or make you feel uncomfortable, turn the page. In essence, you have become your own remote control.

Contained herein is the fuel for many a raucus kitchen table debate or in-depth dorm discussion. Just open up the cover and begin to read out loud. People can't help but respond. Now you're talking!

How to Use This Book

Prepare to test your knowledge of everything you never wanted to know about sex. Contained herein are hundreds of bawdy, but informative odds and ends designed to stimulate the adult...mind.

The information contained in this book is meant to be shared with others in open discussion. However, the real fun begins when you test each other's knowledge of the sexually irrelevant and erotically insignificant.

Pass the book around and take turns attempting to answer various questions. Keep in mind, however, that the truth is often stranger than fiction. So, choose your answers wisely.

You will find the correct answers listed in alphabetical order by title in the back of the book.

If you can't find a crowd to share this book, it makes for great bathroom reading.

MORE CLOVES!

(True or False)

In order to bring in a larger crop of cloves, the men of the South Pacific island of Amboyna ejaculate on the crops immediately after planting has taken place.

AYE AYE SIR

(True or False)

British Admiral Horatio Nelson often referred to his mistress's genitals as, "His little thatched cottage."

SIEG HEIL

(True or False)

One of Adolf Hitler's many bizarre sexual preferences involved a woman urinating on his head.

OH UNCLE MILTY!

(True or False)

Once upon a time, when legendary comedian Milton Berle was challenged to a locker room contest to determine who had the largest penis, a friend advised him to, "Just take out enough to win."

DUBIOUS HONOR

The largest vagina in the animal kingdom is found in the...

a) Whale.
b) Elephant.
c) Gorilla.

OFF THE SHOULDER

(True or False)

In 1452, some women wore a knot over their left shoulder to indicate they were virgins.

THE HARD WAY

(True or False)

Crabs always copulate face to face.

THE EMPEROR HAS NO...

(True or False)

At the time of his death, Napoleon's penis was reported to be approximately two inches long.

STAND AT ATTENTION

Turkish soldiers have been known to have their first sexual experience with...

a) Towels.

b) Vegetables.

c) Chickens.

HANDY MAN

(True or False)

Truman Capote once said, "The good thing about masturbation is that you don't have to beg for it."

BEE MINE

(True or False)

After a male bee copulates, his penis breaks off and he bleeds to death.

HOLD THAT KIELBASA

(True or False)

In Krakow, Poland, the law states that the third time you are caught having sex with an animal, you must be shot in the head.

EAR YE! EAR YE!

(True or False)

In 1529, Cardinal Wolsey was accused of giving Henry VIII syphilis by whispering in his ear.

RABBIT'S FOOT

(True or False)

Before mating, the last thing most male rabbits do to the female is chew on her foot.

SAY WHAT?

(True or False)

In Willowdale, Oregon, it is illegal for a man to talk dirty to his wife while having sex with her.

PRIME CUT

(True or False)

In 1790's London, the castration of a sexual offender was performed by the pig butcher.

MASTER STROKE

"Don't knock masturbation. It's sex with someone I love," is a quote from...

    a) Robin Williams.
    b) Madonna.
    c) Woody Allen.

I TOAD YOU SO

(True or False)

In 95 AD, it was believed that a woman could be safe from conception for a year if she spat into a frog's mouth.

EDUCATION COUNTS

(True or False)

According to Kinsey, better educated men have higher sperm counts than less educated men.

MAKE MINE PISTACHIO

(True or False)

The Kama Sutra claims that penises come in three different sizes and flavors.

GETTING A LITTLE BEHIND

(True or False)

The ideal sexual position for a man with a small penis is doggie style.

HOW RUDE

(True or False)

In Jamaica, doing a "rudeness" with a "teapot" refers to French kissing.

THE BARD

Shakespeare once referred to the female genitals as...

a) "Lovely Ophelia."
b) "Ye damned spots."
c) "Charged chambers."

TOE THE LINE

(True or False)

During the Renaissance, there were many paintings of naked women, but artists were expressly forbidden to show a woman's bare feet or toes.

LISTEN UP

(True or False)

The 1950's expression, "talking to the canoe driver," referred to male masturbation.

WHEN HAIRY MET ARI

When it came to pubic hair, the Ancient Greeks preferred their women...

a) Bushy.

b) Bare.

c) Braided.

WHO LEFT THE SEAT UP?

(True or False)

A scoptophiliac can become sexually aroused by a toilet seat.

PRETTY IN PINK

(True or False)

Bette Midler once walked down Sunset Blvd. wearing nothing but a pink satin ribbon.

CHILD'S PLAY

(True or False)

Sigmund Freud claimed that if you play with a child in your dreams, it represents your desire to deflower a virgin.

BARNACLE BUILT FOR TWO

(True or False)

The penis of a barnacle is 100 times longer than its body.

GOOD VIBRATIONS

In order to make themselves more pleasur-able to women, some men in Sumatra...

a) Use splints to extend their length.
b) Teach themselves to vibrate.
c) Insert small stones into the tip of their penises.

DR. NO

(True or False)

Amongst professional men, the highest rate of impotency is found in elderly doctors.

G'DAY MATE

(True or False)

The men of the Walibri tribe of Australia greet visiting tribesmen by ejaculating.

CUT IT OUT

According to medical science, two of the four degrees of castration are...

a) Stoned and Tail-less.

b) Zipped and tucked.

c) Half geld and Grand geld.

QUITE A STRETCH

According to Kinsey, the number of men who can successfully perform oral sex on themselves is...

a) 1 in 100.

b) 2 in 1000.

c) None.

SLEEPING BEAUTY

A somnophiliac becomes sexually aroused while...

a) Going for long periods without sleep.

b) Sleepwalking.

c) Fondling a sleeping stranger.

DOWN FOR THE COUNT

A man's sperm count is actually reduced while he is...

a) Eating garlic.

b) Taking a bath.

c) Watching television.

PORKIN' BEANS

(True or False)

When an ancient Roman was "Feeling his beans," he was actually fondling breasts.

TALK ABOUT FRIGIDITY

(True or False)

The male penguin usually has only one orgasm per year.

HARD TO BEAT

Long Dong Silver won the all time porn star penis length derby with a member that measured...

a) 13 inches long.

b) 19 inches long.

c) 24 inches long.

FATHER'S DAY

(True or False)

If a Hottentot wife gave birth to twins, the tribe elders would cut off one of the father's testicles.

PAP TEST

(True or False)

In 18th century England, the term "pap-mouth" referred to oral sex.

LOVE THAT TIE

(True or False)

According to historians, the first people to worship the phallus were the Norwegians.

All WASHED UP

The President who claimed that the best time for sex was "In the afternoon, after coming out of the shower," was...

a) Ronald Reagan.

b) John F Kennedy.

c) George Bush.

GOOD DEAL

(True or False)

The Tarot card which supposedly predicts mutual orgasm is called, "The Wheel of Fortune."

THE LITTLE RASCALS

(True or False)

In England, around 1800, a "rascal" was another term for a male prostitute.

MOUTHING OFF

The first state to de-criminalize oral sex was...

a) Nevada.

b) Illinois.

c) Texas.

WHIPPED CREAM

(True or False)

Astrologers say that a good way to arouse a Leo is to use a whip.

TO BEE OR NOT TO BEE

(True or False)

In the 13th century, St. Albert the Great claimed that to prevent pregnancy, a woman should eat bees.

MONKEYING AROUND

During their mating ritual, male squirrel monkeys...

a) Spank each other's bottom.

b) Urinate in each other's face.

c) Suck their own toes.

BOX LUNCH

(True or False)

The "Happy Hooker" reported that her peak business hours were between 12-1 PM.

SURPRISE

(True or False)

In 1974, Prince Charles ordered two chastity belts and gave them as gifts to his sisters.

HOW ABOUT SOME FUR-PLAY

If you made love like a mink, it would look like you were...
- a) Fighting.
- b) Dancing.
- c) Dead.

I'LL FOLLOW YOU ANY-WHERE

(True or False)

Astrologers say that, aside from the genitals, the most sensitive erogenous zone for an Aquarian is the ear.

WHAT A BOAR

(True or False)

The length of time it takes a boar to deliver its full load of semen is 10 minutes.

LOTUS ENTERTAIN YOU

(True or False)

The Kama Sutra tells us that if the "Yoni Juices" of a woman resemble a "Lotus Flower," she will have a medium sized vagina.

MIND OVER MAMMARIES

(True or False)

Dr. Richard Willard of Indianapolis has successfully enlarged female breasts from 2 to 4 inches by using hypnosis.

FIDDLING AROUND

(True or False)

After first dressing them in his dead wife's clothes, Roman Emperor Nero would make love to his palace guards.

TOUCHY SITUATION

The human penis is about as sensitive as...

a) An ear lobe.

b) An eyelid.

c) The sole of the foot.

MERRY QUEEN OF SCOTS

(True or False)

In 1700's Scotland, a "Tirly Wirly" was another name for a homosexual.

SHORT MEMORY

"It lasted about a minute and a half, and that included buying the dress," describes the first sexual experience of...

a) Cathy Lee Gifford.

b) Erma Bombeck.

c) Joan Rivers.

PERFECT SCORE

According to a *Playboy Magazine* survey, the number of women who reach orgasm every time is...

a) 25%.

b) 40%.

c) 80%.

MAKING A PROPHET

The prophet Isaiah referred to pubic hair as "The...

a) "Burning bush."

b) "Hair of the feet."

c) "Gateway to Heaven."

KEEP THE TIP

(True or False)

If a young boy of the Kuoma Tribe of New Guinea is caught with an erection, he is immediately circumcised.

SALAMATERNITY

Alpine Salamanders remain pregnant for a little over three...

a) Years.

b) Months.

c) Days.

BREAST MAN

(True or False)

The affliction, Gynecomastia, is an abnormal enlargement of the male breasts.

BLOWING IN THE WIND

(True or False)

According to Aristotle, if a woman had sex while the wind was blowing North, she would miscarry.

BRUSH STROKES

It is rumored that Renoir painted his nudes by using...

a) Brushes made of pubic hair.

b) His penis.

c) Paint mixed with his own semen.

OOPS

(True or False)

According to superstition, the spilling of salt is bad luck because it symbolizes premature ejaculation.

TWO FOR THE PRICE OF ONE

(True or False)

The female butterfly has two vaginas.

CHUG A LUG

(True or False)

To increase their sexual ability, Apache Indians would drink a potion made from ground buffalo testicles.

WHITE OUT

(True or False)

Until recently on the island of Bali, the only sexual taboo was to have sex with an albino.

SEE YOU IN SEPTEMBER

(True or False)

According to the Ayatollah Khomieni, a husband must have sexual relations with his wife at least once every four months.

AN OUNCE OF PREVENTION

In order to prevent nocturnal emissions, Victorian men would...

a) Wear tight underwear.

b) Sleep standing up.

c) Tie strings around their genitals.

MOBY'S DICK

Aristotle Onassis once used the skins of Sperm Whale testicles to...

a) Make custom condoms.

b) Upholster the bar stools on his yacht.

c) Make slippers.

PRISON IS NO BALL

(True or False)

According to a study done in a state penitentiary, men would live 13 years longer without testicles.

THREE'S COMPANY

(True or False)

According to Freud, if you dream about the number 3, you are actually dreaming about a menage a trois.

GROPING IN THE DARK

Shakespeare once referred to sexual intercourse as...

a) A singing in the loins.

b) Groping for trouts.

c) A prickling pair.

LADIES AND GENITALMEN

(True or False)

According to superstition, placing a ring on a bride's finger symbolizes her husband's possession of her genitals.

HOLE IN THE HEAD

(True or False)

The female snail has her vagina in her head.

AN AFFAIR TO REMEMBER

(True or False)

To have an affair with a married man, a voodoo priestess will sew his name in a chicken bladder.

PUT WHAT WHERE?

"The only unnatural sex act is that which you cannot perform," is a quote from...

a) Madonna.
b) Benjamin Franklin.
c) Dr. Alfred Kinsey.

A PLACE OF WORSHIP

(True or False)

In the 3rd century, theologian Tertullian described woman as, "A temple built on a sewer."

SHELL GAME

During erection, the penis of the turtle...

a) Turns inside out.

b) Turns bright red.

c) Swims ahead of its body.

COLD FEET

(True or False)

Elvis Presley was sexually turned-off by women with big feet.

TIME FOR A RAISE

(True or False)

In a recent survey of America's intimate sex habits, most American women fantasized about having sex with their boss.

BEDSIDE MANNER

In 1810, European physicians cured male masturbation by...

a) Cutting the tip off the penis.

b) Severing the nerves of the penis.

c) Sewing fingers together.

MONKEY BUSINESS

(True or False)

The spider monkey's penis is covered with spaghetti-like tendrils.

SIGN IN PLEASE

(True or False)

According to handwriting experts, if you leave your d's and r's open, you are most likely to be multi-orgasmic.

HOLY PLAYBOY?

(True or False)

The world's largest collection of sexually-orientated literature is located in the Vatican library in Rome.

NUNSENSE

In order to insure the chastity of nuns, St. Jerome forbade the eating of...

a) Beans.

b) Bratwurst.

c) Cucumbers.

FOUNDING PHILANDERER

(True or False)

Benjamin Franklin recommended having sex with older women because they would remember you in their wills.

ANY WAY YOU LOOK AT IT

In ancient Greek, the word "gonorrhea" literally meant...

a) The tankard is leaking.

b) Shriveled grapes.

c) Flow of seed.

DON'T FRET

(True or False)

According to an ancient Arabian sex manual, a woman with a large vagina will also have feet like a guitar.

IN THE STARS

(True or False)

Astrologers say that a Taurus can be sexually aroused by tickling the bottom of his or her feet.

YOUR PART'S BEEN CUT

(True or False)

To stop them from taking advantage of their female fans, actors in Ancient Rome were castrated.

PUPPY CHOW

(True or False)

To be assured that her breasts were emptied of milk, a Victorian mother would sometimes use a suckling puppy.

LITTLE DEVILS

(True or False)

When sperm cells were first discovered in the 17th century, some thought they were creatures of the devil.

GOTTA GO

(True or False)

According to research, immediately after intercourse, most people go to the bathroom.

EASY COME, EASY GO

The now defunct rock group that named themselves after the contents of an ejaculation was...

a) Cream.

b) Lovin' Spoonful.

c) 10CC.

COMINGS AND GOINGS

"There will be sex after death. We just won't be able to feel it," is a quote from...

a) Roseanne Barr.
b) Lily Tomlin.
c) Pee Wee Herman.

LOOK ON THE BRIGHT SIDE

Castrated males rarely get...

a) Hemorrhoids.
b) Gout.
c) Dandruff.

DINNER DATE

(True or False)

According to the Ayatollah Khomeini, it is acceptable to have sex with a lamb, but a mortal sin to eat it afterwards.

I'M STUMPED

To become sexually aroused, an acromophiliac must imagine that his partner is ...

a) An amputee.

b) An acrobat.

c) A farmer.

EAU DE TOILET

(True or False)

In order to prevent pregnancy, some women in the Dark Ages wore a special perfume made from the secretions of skunk glands.

BALLED UP

(True or False)

Captain Cook, Beethoven and Mussolini each had undescended testicles.

FUTURE SHOCK

The Tarot card which indicates the loss of sexual power is called...

a) *The Tower.*
b) *The Hanged Man.*
c) *Death.*

I'VE GOT A SECRETION

When ready to mate, an elephant's glands secrete a gooey liquid called...

a) Tuskid.
b) Muskaphant.
c) Musth.

WEIGHT UP

(True or False)

Hippocrates suggested that to avoid getting pregnant, a woman should put on weight.

TICKED OFF

Because the tick has no penis, it copulates with its...

    a) Tail.
    b) Nose.
    c) Wings.

LOWER PLEASE

(True or False)

In 1709, the widespread incidence of infertility was attributed to singing during sex.

COVER UP

In order to cover his genitals while posing as a "Cosmopolitan" centerfold, Burt Reynolds used...

a) His arm.
b) The racing form.
c) A brown derby.

AS LOOSE AS...

In 19th century England, the term "goose grease" referred to...

a) The money paid to a prostitute.
b) Semen.
c) Vaginal secretions.

SOUNDS FISHY TO ME

(True or False)

To help control the quality of trout on a trout farm, breeders created trout without sex organs.

FOOTBALLING

When asked if a homosexual could find happiness in the NFL, Bubba Smith once replied...

a) "Sure sweety."
b) "Not if he comes looking for it in my room."
c) "Go ask Howard Cosell."

BURNT PIECE

(True or False)

One of the most painful masturbation techniques on record involved the use of a toaster.

LOWE LIFE

(True or False)

Rob Lowe supposedly tried to pick-up Melissa Gilbert by telling her he wanted to "Check *Nasty* for snake bites."

THE CURE-ALL

(True or False)

In ancient Babylon, a cure for impotence was to eat dates dipped in bull's urine.

WHEN IN FRANCE

According to French medieval law, a woman was guilty of adultery if she...

a) Drank from a strange man's goblet.
b) Kissed someone other than her husband.
c) Shaved under her arms.

OVAR EASY

Removal of the ovaries is sometimes referred to as an...

a) Oopherectomy.

b) Overoutomy.

c) O.U.T.

LAID TO REST

(True or False)

Actress Sarah Bernhardt was fond of making love in a silk-lined coffin.

GET THE POINT

(True or False)

In order to attract a mate, the male porcupine will rub her with his quill.

MAYBE IT'S ANEMIA

(True or False)

At one time, Transylvanian Gypsies blamed a wife's lack of children on her pre-marital affair with a vampire.

VILE CONTENTS

Semen for artificial insemination is usually stored in...

a) Condoms.

b) Plastic straws.

c) Tupperware.

BRAGGING RIGHTS

(True or False)

The largest average penis among primates is found in the gorilla.

MR. RUBBER

The condom was invented by...

  a) Benjamin Franklin.

  b) Louis Pasteur.

  c) Colonel Condom.

ET TU

Taken from the Latin, the term "masturbation" literally means to...

a) Pump the handle.
b) Polish the knob.
c) Pollute one's self.

TENDER MOMENTS

(True or False)

Once upon a time in Siberia, if a woman threw freshly killed lice at a man, it indicated she was ready for marriage.

POUNDING THE PELTS

(True or False)

Mink copulate in a matter of seconds.

GIDDY UP!

It was once believed that the testicle of an ass could increase sexual desire if you...

    a) Wore it on your wrist.
    b) Ate it.
    c) Fondled it.

GLOOMY FORECAST

(True or False)

Queen Marie Therese of France blamed her black child on the predominantly overcast weather during her pregnancy.

SAY AHHH!

(True or False)

Aside from the genitals and breasts, the only other body part that swells during intercourse is your tongue.

DIAL 911

(True or False)

In Tremonton, Utah, it is against the law to have sex in an ambulance.

IN A PICKLE

According to some authorities, if you dream about many cucumbers, you may be dreaming about...

a) Masturbation.
b) Group sex.
c) Homosexuality.

BREASTS OF BURDEN

(True or False)

In order to keep their breasts out of the way while working in the fields, some African women throw them over their shoulders.

I GIVE GREAT FIGARO

An 18th century French prostitute was not punished if she chose to...

a) Enter a convent.
b) Shave her head.
c) Join the Paris Opera.

CLOSET LIBERAL

(True or False)

U.S. President Warren G. Harding was fond of having sexual liaisons in a White House closet.

ONE HUMP OR TWO

According to Ancient Jewish custom, a camel driver must have sex with his wife...

a) Once every 30 days.
b) On each high holiday.
c) Before he feeds his camel.

DEFLOWERED CHILD

(True or False)

According to ancient Jewish law, a virgin had to be married on a Wednesday because the the high court met on Thursdays, thus allowing new husbands to file their non-viginity complaints immediately.

THE NATIONAL PASTIME

(True or False)

Over 80 percent of all Americans engage in oral sex.

SHARE AND SHARE ALIKE

(True or False)

According to an Arab legend, King Solomon refused to bed the Queen of Sheba until she had sex with his brother.

WAIT UP

Newlyweds of the Dani tribe of New Guinea have their first sex after waiting a period of...

a) 3 months.
b) 15 minutes.
c) 2 years.

TALKING TRASH

(True or False)

A poll asking Cleveland residents if they considered pornography to be trash was conducted by city garbage collectors.

OH GOD

(True or False)

The Egyptian god, Osiris, was usually depicted as having three penises.

I LOVE EWE

In Ancient Rome, anyone caught having sex with an animal was...

a) Branded like cattle.
b) Forced to pay a tax.
c) Beheaded.

LUG NUTS

(True or False)

Compared to its body weight, the creature with the largest testicles is the Cockroach.

IT'S A RAP

If you are a rapophiliac, you become sexually aroused by...

a) Loud music.

b) Being tied up.

c) Terrified resistance.

NO HORSING AROUND

In Newcastle, Wyoming, there is a law that prohibits having sex...

a) On Sunday.

b) On horseback.

c) In a meat freezer.

COMING MOTHER

(True or False)

Nearly two-thirds of all Americans have had sex in their parent's home while their parents were in the house.

FAMILY AFFAIR

(True or False)

If you practice endogamy, you will only marry someone from within your own family.

JUNEAU THAT?

(True or False)

The state with the highest reported rape rate is Alaska.

BONE-APART

(True or False)

At a 1969 auction, $39,000 was paid for Napoleon's severed penis.

PICK A WINNER

(True or False)

Supposedly, a man's nose is directly related to the size of his penis.

FUR-GET IT

(True or False)

In Peru, it is against the law for a man to copulate with a female alpaca.

IN LIKE FLYNN

Actor Errol Flynn was reputed to have had a homosexual affair with...

a) Tyrone Power.

b) Truman Capote.

c) Howard Hughes.

YOU PLAY, YOU PAY

In the 12th Century, a convicted adulterer had to pay a fine which was called...

a) Penile Restitution.

b) Carnal Taxation.

c) Lecherwhite.

THAT'S A LOTTA BULL

(True or False)

The semen from one single bull orgasm can artificially inseminate as many as 300 cows.

FETA ATTRACTION

(True or False)

To increase their sexual ability, ancient Greeks would drink a potion made from feta cheese and bull sperm.

HANGING AROUND

In England in the late 1700's, a "rantallion" was a man...

a) Who was hung like a horse.

b) Whose scrotum hung below his penis.

c) Who had an orgasm when watching a hanging.

SWAPPING SEBUM

A substance called sebum is transferred between lovers by...

a) Kissing.

b) Intercourse.

c) Sweating.

IT'S A BALL

(True or False)

Clinton, Montana is the site of a banquet called, "The Testicle Festival."

UP ALL NIGHT

Supposedly, Sir Isaac Newton's acute insomnia was caused by...

a) His lifelong virginity.

b) Syphilis.

c) A steady stream of prostitutes.

THE RIGHT ANGLE

(True or False)

In the 17th century, doctors claimed that for a woman to conceive, she should lie on her right side and avoid sneezing.

FOLLOW THE LEADER

(True or False)

Ancient Greek prostitutes marked the way to the brothel by embossing the words, "follow me," on the back of their cloaks.

THE TIME OF YOUR LIFE

In the course of a man's entire lifetime, the actual time he spends experiencing sexual climax is approximately...

a) 2 hours.

b) 9 hours.

c) 3 days.

PENILE INSTITUTION

In 18th century Naples, the largest public phallic symbol was a statue nicknamed, "The...

a) "Long Tower."

b) "Great Toe of Corso."

c) "Dictator."

PIG IN A POKE

(True or False)

The penis of the pig is similar in action to that of a jackhammer.

YESSIR ARABFAT

(True or False)

According to an ancient Arabian sex manual, to prolong an erection, rub the penis with the fat from a melted camel hump.

BEDTIME STORY

(True or False)

A narratophiliac wants to have sex while someone reads to him.

I GUESS THEY HAD NO BANANAS

(True or False)

The decoration on many Greek vases of the 5th Century BC featured women carrying baskets full of dildos.

EARLY BIRD

(True or False)

Premature ejaculation is caused by an overly sensitive penis.

BEATING AROUND THE BUSHMEN

Male Bushmen of the Kalahari Desert have penises that are always...

a) Dripping.
b) Semi-erect.
c) Tied in a knot.

THE FRENCH DISCONNECTION

(True or False)

After French President Faure died while copulating in a brothel, his penis had to be surgically removed from the lady in question.

FLOUR CHILD

(True or False)

If an Australian Aboriginal woman had a child that was half white, the tribe would blame it on eating the white man's flour.

COME CLEAN

(True or False)

During lovemaking, the male rhinoceros stays mounted on the female while she bathes.

HAPPY TROILS TO YOU

If you practice Troilism, you become sexually aroused by...

a) Wearing expensive jewelry.

b) The danger of being discovered.

c) Being the third party in a threesome.

FRIENDS, ROMANS AND ?

Of the first 15 Emperors of Rome, Claudius was the only...

a) Heterosexual.

b) Transvestite.

c) Necrophiliac.

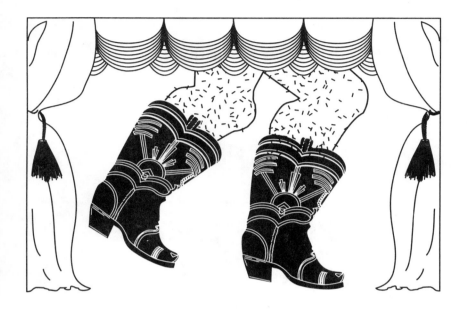

PUSS 'N BOOTS

"He doesn't even take his boots off," was a lady's sexual criticism of...

a) Adolf Hitler.
b) John Wayne.
c) Garth Brooks.

BAT HER UP

Male bats have sex while...

a) Hanging upside down by their toes.
b) In mid air.
c) The female is sleeping.

PETER PRINCIPLE

Amongst professional men, the lowest rate of impotence is for...

a) Politicians.
b) Dentists.
c) Elderly clergy.

LOCK-HER ROOM

(True or False)

The last chastity belts were hand made in England in the mid 1970's.

MR. COFFEE

(True or False)

In the 19th century, gynecologists believed that a man would become impotent if he drank 10 cups of coffee per day.

YOU'D BE BLUE TOO

The testicles of a Blue Whale weigh approximately...

a) 5 pounds.
b) 110 pounds.
c) 740 pounds.

WHAT'S YOUR SIGN

According to the Gay sex signaling code, if you wear or display a purple handkerchief, you're into...

a) Heavy S & M.
b) Body Piercing.
c) Monogamy.

KNOT FUNNY

(True or False)

The men of a tribe in Uganda elongate their penises enough to tie them in knots by having their fellow tribesmen pull on them in a daily ritual.

LETTER PERFECT

If a female has school-type handwriting with narrow loops and letters, she probably...

a) Is hot to trot.
b) Doesn't enjoy sex.
c) Is a closet lesbian.

HERE COMES SANTA CLAUS

The Christmas plant that was once believed to promote great sexual power was...

a) Mistletoe.
b) Poinsettia.
c) Balsam.

WELL HUNG

(True or False)

Most eunuchs in ancient China put their severed testicles in a jar and carried them around their necks.

AND THE BAND PLAYED ON

(True or False)

The 19th century slang term meaning "sex" that became the name for a type of popular music was "ragtime."

MISSION CONTROL

(True or False)

In Ancient Greece, as a method of birth control, women were advised by physicians to insert a handful of Greek olives.

SO SIOUX ME

A 1947 ad, featuring a Native American couple in bed, had the caption...

a) "A buck well spent on a Springmaid sheet."

b) "Me have no reservations on a Springmaid sheet."

c) "Me know how. Want to know when."

79

PEE-NALIZED

(True or False)

The Hebrew Talmud forbids men to hold their penises while urinating unless they wear gloves.

ELBOW GREASE

(True or False)

Astrologers say that the most sensitive erogenous zone for a Virgo, other than the genitals, is the elbow.

LADY BYRD SINGS THE BLUES

(True or False)

The US President who claimed that if he went too long without sex, he got a headache was Lyndon Johnson.

WHORE-MONAL THERAPY

According to Aristotle, most whores do not get pregnant because...

a) They develop an immunity.
b) Their vagina is too slippery to hold semen.
c) Evil spirits kill the seed.

FINAL CURTAIN

(True or False)

Former Vice President Nelson Rockefeller dropped dead while watching a strip tease show.

SMALL PROBLEM

(True or False)

The Kama Sutra tells us that a man with a five inch penis will have a lonely life.

SNAKE EYES

(True or False)

To protect the wearer from the evil eye, the men of the Mambas tribe of the New Hebrides often wrap their penises in snakeskin.

SNAP, CRACKLE, POPLESS

"I seem to get along very well without orgasms," was a quote from...

a) Jane Quayle.
b) Tennessee Williams.
c) John Wayne Bobbitt.

BOILING MAD

(True or False)

An ancient Greek method of birth control was to immerse the man's penis in boiling water.

INCH WORM

(True or False)

The smallest penis ever recorded, with testes and normal functioning, was only one half inch in length.

MEASURING TOOL

(True or False)

The longest penis in history, to be clinically verified, measured seventeen inches long.

OH SWELL

(True or False)

When a man gets Gonorrhea, his testicles can swell to the size of a grapefruit.

RUB A DUB DUB

Astrologers say that an Aries will become sexually aroused if you massage his or her...

a) Toes.
b) Kneecaps.
c) Scalp.

FROM HERE TO MATERNITY

(True or False)

According to an early 1900's sex manual, if you have sex with a pregnant woman, the baby will be born blind.

A PERFECT 10

(True or False)

The Kama Sutra claimed that a man with a ten inch penis would be reckless and lazy.

PICTURE THIS

The only X-rated film to receive the Best Picture Oscar was...

a) "The Last Tango In Paris."

b) "Midnight Cowboy."

c) "A Streetcar Named Desire."

DIDDLER ON THE ROOF

According to ancient Jewish law, a man could be put to death for having sex with his mother, having sex with another male and also for...

a) Having sex with an animal.

b) Having sex with a menstruating woman.

c) Refusing to be circumcised.

GOING TO POT

(True or False)

An apotemnophiliac can become sexually aroused at the sight of kitchen utensils.

TICKLE TICKLE

In the mid 1600's, a "tickle-gizzard" was another name for...

a) Female pubic hair.

b) A prostitute.

c) A penis.

BOY OH BOY

(True or False)

In order to be aroused enough to make love to their wives, ancient Spartans often dressed them up like boys.

WORN OUT

In Ancient Greece, Discorides believed that a person could be made infertile by wearing...

a) Red.

b) Too much jewelry.

c) Asparagus.

REAL HOOFER

(True or False)

Welsh ponies masturbate with their hooves.

FALX OF THE ROMAN EMPIRE

(True or False)

One of the popular names of the penis in Roman times was "falx," which literally meant "sickle."

HONEY, LET ME DO THE WASH

(True or False)

A mysophiliac can become sexually aroused by dirty underwear.

UNLAWFUL ENTRY

According to the Koran, the punishment for stealing another man's wife is...

a) Death.
b) Castration.
c) The confiscation of his livestock.

BRAZIL NUTS

The men of the Xavanta tribe in Brazil believe that they increase their sexual potency by...

a) Never shaving.
b) Eating python skin.
c) Wearing red plugs in their ears.

SHARK ATTACK

(True or False)

Male Bottle-nosed Dolphins sometimes masturbate by rubbing against a passing shark.

BELLY FLOP

(True or False)

According to an ancient Arabian sex manual, a woman with a large vagina will have a belly like a withered date.

OCTOPUSSY

The vagina of the female octopus is located in...

a) One of her two crotches.

b) Her nose.

c) The tip of a tentacle.

RUNNING MATE

(True or False)

James Buchanan, the 15th President of the United States, was rumored to have had a homosexual affair with his Vice President, William Rufus DeVane King.

FROTT WITH PERIL

If you are a frotteurist, you become sexually aroused by...

a)   Rubbing against strangers in a crowd.
b)   The smell of cheap perfume on a prostitute.
c)   Exposing yourself to young children.

OVER-EXPOSURE

A flasher becomes sexually aroused by...

a) The shock of the victim.
b) The fear of being caught.
c) Wind currents.

SKIN MAGAZINE

(True or False)

The magazine devoted to men who wish to reverse their circumcisions is called, *Foreskin Quarterly.*

COME TO YOUR SENSES

The primary sensory signal to male mammals that a female is ready to mate is her...

    a) Scent.
    b) Breathing.
    c) Protests.

ALL CHOKED UP

(True or False)

During sex, the male lizard chokes the female while inserting his two penises.

HAIL TO THE CHIEF

According to one of his many mistresses, JFK's most outstanding characteristic in bed was...

    a) His sexual know-how.
    b) The size of his penis.
    c) His sense of humor.

MAKING A LONG STORY SHORT

(True or False)

The fairy tale that supposedly represents a boy's castration of his father is, "The Three Little Pigs."

BREAKFAST OF CHAMPIONS

In 18th century England, a common aphrodisiac was to eat the...

a)   Afterbirth of a cow.

b)   Brain of a dove.

c)   Testicles of a goat.

CHOCK FULL'O NUTS

(True or False)

Rapper Marky Mark is reputed to have three testicles.

CAPITAL OFFENSE

(True or False)

In Washington D.C., there is a law that prohibits having sex doggie style.

'TIS THE SEASON

(True or False)

According to research, the peak human mating season is the Christmas Holidays.

MODEL BEHAVIOR

(True or False)

It is widely believed that Leonardo da Vinci was a virgin.

CLASSIC TAIL

The longest orgasm described in a classic work of literature occupies 30 pages of ...

a) *Ulysses.*

b) *Lady Chatterly's Lover.*

c) *A Tale of Two Cities.*

EBONY & IVORY

(True or False)

The average Caucasion penis measured by Dr.Kinsey was 4 inches long, while the average Negro penis was seven inches long.

BONUS

Rams and goats get a slight erection each time they...

a) Butt horns.

b) Eat.

c) Urinate.

BREAST MILK

(True or False)

According to a Southern folk tale, a man who drinks lots of milk will grow women's breasts.

OFF WITH HER HEAD

(True or False)

When Cecil B DeMille said, "This book contains more sex and violence than I could ever portray on the screen," he was referring to "Alice In Wonderland."

MIND OF ITS OWN

(True or False)

In some species of Octopus, the penis detaches and copulates with the female.

EAT YOUR HEART OUT

(True or False)

In ancient Babylonia, a cure for impotence was to eat the heart of a beheaded partridge.

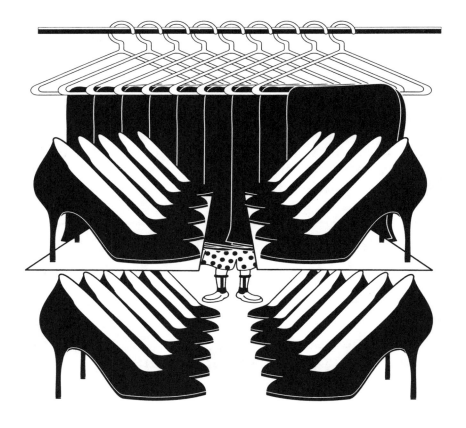

SHORT STORY

(True or False)

One of the most unbelievable sexual rumors involved an affair between Imelda Marcos and *Fantasy Island's* Herve Villachez.

KLIS ME GOODBYE

If you are a klismaphiliac, you become sexually aroused when you're given...

a) A passing grade.
b) An enema.
c) Bad news.

EXCREMENT HAPPENS

In 100 AD, the punishment for a Teutonic prostitute was...

a) Suffocation in excrement.
b) Female circumcision.
c) To be tattooed with the letter L.

SAFE BET

(True or False)

The state with the lowest reported rape rate is Nevada.

ROSEY PALM

(True or False)

According to Sigmund Freud, if a man dreams about a rose, he may actually be dreaming about masturbating.

BOBBY'S GIRL

(True or False)

A woman claiming to be Bobby Kennedy's mistress described him as, "very serious and deliberate in the sack."

LITTLE BUGGER

Because the male Bedbug's penis is so small that he can't reach the female's vagina, during the mating ritual he...

a) Stabs it through her back.
b) Crawls completely inside of her.
c) Stands on another male's back.

TWISTED SISTER

The number of lovemaking positions listed in the Kama Sutra is...

a) 84.
b) 921.
c) 27.

REDHEAD

The penis of the Red Squirrel greatly resembles a...

a) Twig.
b) Bing cherry.
c) Long piece of thread.

GET A HOLD OF YOURSELF

(True or False)

In Clinton, Oklahoma, there is a law that prohibits masturbating while watching two people have sex in a car.

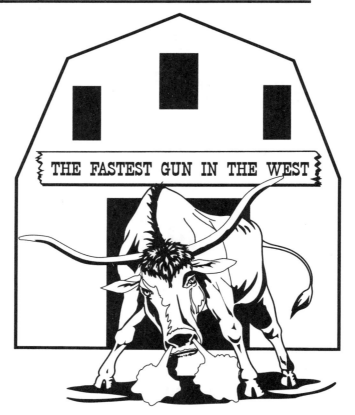

THE FASTEST GUN IN THE WEST

WAS IT GOOD FOR YOU?

(True or False)

A bull copulates in one thrust, which lasts less than a second.

PUBIC ENEMY

Someone suffering from gymnophobia finds it difficult to have sex because of an irrational fear of...

a) Body odor.
b) Pubic hair.
c) Being seen naked.

STRIP SEARCH

In 1895, the Strip Tease was invented because of a dancer's...

a) Search for a flea.
b) Urgent need to urinate.
c) Poison Ivy infection.

I'VE BEEN SLIMED!

(True or False)

Great Gray Slugs copulate while dangling from a rope of their own slime.

VIII IS ENOUGH

(True or False)

Pope Innocent the VIII was called, "Innocent the Honest," because he admitted that he liked boys.

HEAD WOUND

If you were standing naked among a group of ancient Greek athletes and you were circumcised, you would be...

a) Put to death.
b) Proud.
c) Embarrassed.

WHATEVER HAPPENED TO GOING BLIND?

(True or False)

Aside from painful itching and tumors of the bladder, an 18th century sex manual also listed a possible symptom of masturbation as, "warts on the palms of the hands."

LIP SERVICE

(True or False)

Because goodbye kisses caused a traffic jam at an Illinois train station, a sign was posted which read, "No Couples Allowed."

HARD TO BELIEVE

The Greek god, known for his perpetual erection, was...

a) Adonis.
b) Erectis.
c) Priapus.

SAFE SEX

Ancient Chinese women felt safe from pregnancy after...

a) Binding their abdomens with silk.
b) Burning wormwood leaves in their navels.
c) Eating wan ton with dog meat.

GET MY GOAT

(True or False)

In some parts of India, it is legal for a woman to marry a goat.

ROCKS OF AGES

(True or False)

One popular name for testicles in Roman times was "mala," which literally meant, "boulders."

DE PAIN! DE PAIN!

"I like to hurt women when I make love to them...I like to see them bleed," is a quote from...

a) Jack Nicholson.
b) Charles Manson.
c) Mike Tyson.

SMOKIN'

In 18th century Britain, "to make the chimney smoke," meant to...

a) Ejaculate.
b) Give a woman an orgasm.
c) Pass gas.

JACK THE ZIPPER

(True or False)

When Dean Martin said, "His zipper should be left to the Smithsonian," he was referring to the sexual exploits of John F. Kennedy.

INSIDE INFORMATION

(True or False)

Whips and riding crops are often made from "pizzles," which are the internal sex organs of a goat.

SHORT HAND

(True or False)

According to handwriting experts, if you have sharp, angular lower loops, you tend to be quick to climax.

DOWN THE HATCH

As an ancient form of contraception, the women in some mid-eastern tribes would swallow...

a)   Their own tongues.
b)   Whole figs, dipped in goat urine.
c)   The foam from a camel's mouth.

LAWN JOCKEY

(True or False)

According to the "Gay Handbook," if you wear a green scarf in your right pocket, you like doing it outside.

IT PAYS TO ADVERTISE

Male prostitutes in ancient Rome advertised their occupation by...

a)   Scratching their heads with their middle finger.
b)   Cutting off their middle finger.
c)   Painting their nipples orange.

'TIS BETTER TO GIVE

According to the Bible, David won the hand of King Saul's daughter by making a gift of the...

a) Foreskins of 1000 Philistines.

b) Nipples of his arch enemy.

c) Penis of a kosher goat.

PEEPING TOM

(True or False)

In 1894, Thomas Edison made sexual history by inventing the Peep Show Machine.

THEY'RE OFF

The Greek word "eunuch" literally means...

a) Without manhood.
b) Guardian of the bed.
c) Seedless grape.

COME AGAIN?

Hamsters have been known to copulate as much as 75 times per...

a) Month.
b) Hour.
c) Day.

INCHING ALONG

(True or False)

The penis of an Orangutan, when erect, is bright pink but only 1/2 inch long.

MUSEUM PIECE

The gangster whose 20" penis is rumored to be preserved in the Smithsonian Institute is...

a) John Dillinger.

b) Al Capone.

c) Clyde Barrow.

GRAIN OF TRUTH

(True or False)

According to ancient wisdom, an aging man could be revived sexually by eating wild oats.

THE YOLK'S ON ME

(True or False)

According to some authorities, if a woman dreams about "breaking eggs," she may be dreaming about getting pregnant.

ORGAN-IZED

Shakespeare once referred to the male organ as...

a) Poor Yorick.

b) A bare bodkin.

c) The potato finger.

OAKEY DOKEY

The ancient Teutons believed that all Oak trees were male because...

a) Their sap was white and milky.

b) Their acorns resembled penises.

c) They were so big and erect.

THE ANSWERS

A

ALL CHOKED UP- True

ALL WASHED UP- a) Ronald Reagan

AN AFFAIR TO REMEMBER- True

AN OUNCE OF PREVENTION- c) Tie strings around their genitals

AND THE BAND PLAYED ON- False (It was jazz.)

ANY WAY YOU LOOK AT IT- c) Flow of seed

A PERFECT 10- True

A PLACE OF WORSHIP- True

AS LOOSE AS- c) Vaginal Secretions

AYE AYE SIR- True

B

BALLED UP- False (Each had syphilis.)

BARNACLE BUILT FOR TWO- False (It's only 30 times larger.)

BAT HER UP- a) Hanging upside down by their toes

BEATING AROUND THE BUSHMEN- b) Semi-erect

BEDSIDE MANNER- b) Severing the nerves of the penis

BEDTIME STORY- True

BEE MINE- True

BELLY FLOP- False (It would be like an empty leather bottle.)

BLOWING IN THE WIND- False (She would have a boy.)

BOBBY'S GIRL- False (He was said to be boyish and cheerful in bed.)

BOILING MAD- True

BONE-APART- True

BONUS- C) Urinate

BOX LUNCH- False (It was between 3-4 PM.)

BOY OH BOY- True

BRAGGING RIGHTS- False (Humans have this honor.)

BRAZIL NUTS- c) Wearing red plugs in their ears

BREAKFAST OF CHAMPIONS- b) Brain of a dove

BREAST MAN- True

BREAST MILK- False (He would supposedly ejaculate greater
                                    amounts.)

BREASTS OF BURDEN- True

BRUSH STROKES- b) His penis

BURNT PIECE- False (A vacuum cleaner)

CAPITAL OFFENSE- True

CHILD'S PLAY- False (It represents masturbation.)

CHOCK FULL 'O NUTS- False (He has 3 nipples.)

CHUG A LUG- False (It was made from human excrement.)

CLASSIC TAIL- a) Ulysses

CLOSET LIBERAL- True

COLD FEET- True

COME AGAIN- c) Day

COME CLEAN- False (He stays mounted while his legs swing free off
the ground.)

COME TO YOUR SENSES- a) Scent

COMING MOTHER- True

COMINGS AND GOINGS- b) Lily Tomlin

COVER UP- a) His arm

CUT IT OUT- a) Stoned and Tail-less

DEFLOWERED CHILD- True

DE PAIN! DE PAIN!- c) Mike Tyson

DIAL 911- True

DIDDLER ON THE ROOF- All three (a,b & c)

DINNER DATE- True

DON'T FRET- True

DOWN FOR THE COUNT- b) Taking a hot bath

DOWN THE HATCH- c) The foam from a camel's mouth

DR. NO- True

DUBIOUS HONOR- a) Whale

EAR YE! EAR YE!- True

EARLY BIRD- False (It's caused by a lack of emotional control.)

EASY COME, EASY GO- c) 10CC

EAT YOUR HEART OUT- True

EAU DE TOILET- False (They wore a cat's testicle on their navel.)

EBONY AND IVORY- False (The average Negro penis was 4 1/2" long.)

EDUCATION COUNTS- False (They have more wet dreams.)

ELBOW GREASE- False (It's the stomach.)

ET TU- c) To pollute oneself

EXCREMENT HAPPENS- a) Suffocation in excrement

FALX OF THE ROMAN EMPIRE- True
FAMILY AFFAIR- True
FATHER'S DAY- True
FETA ATTRACTION- False (The milk of an ass and the blood of a bat.)
FIDDLING AROUND- False (He would make love to young boys.)
FINAL CURTAIN- False (He died while having sex.)
FLOUR CHILD- True
FOLLOW THE LEADER- False (It was on the bottom of their shoes.)
FOOTBALLING- b) "Not if he comes looking for it in my room."
FOUNDING PHILANDERER- False (Because they would be so grateful)
FRIENDS, ROMANS AND ?- a) Heterosexual
FROM HERE TO MATERNITY- False (The baby would be epilectic.)
FROTT WITH PERIL- a) Rubbing against strangers
FUR-GET IT- True
FUTURE SHOCK- a) The Tower

G'DAY MATE- False (They shake penises.)
GET A HOLD OF YOURSELF- True
GET MY GOAT- True
GET THE POINT- False (He will spray her with urine.)
GETTING A LITTLE BEHIND- True
GIDDY UP- a) Wore it on your wrist
GLOOMY FORECAST- False (It was blamed on her pet negro dwarf.)
GOING TO POT- False (It is the thought of losing a limb.)
GOOD DEAL- False (It's called, "The Sun.")
GOOD VIBRATIONS- c) Insert small stones
GOTTA GO- False (Most people go to sleep.)
GRAIN OF TRUTH-False (By making love to a virgin.)
GROPING IN THE DARK- b) Groping for trouts

H

HAIL TO THE CHIEF- c) His sense of humor
HANDY MAN- False ("That you don't have to dress up for it.")
HANGING AROUND- b) Whose scrotum hung below his penis
HAPPY TROILS TO YOU- c) Being the 3rd party in a threesome
HARD TO BEAT- b) 19" long
HARD TO BELIEVE- c) Priapus
HEAD WOUND- c) Embarrassed
HERE COMES SANTA CLAUS- a) Mistletoe
HOLD THAT KIELBASA- True

HOLE IN THE HEAD- True
HOLY PLAYBOY?- True
HONEY, LET ME DO THE WASH?- True
HOW ABOUT SOME FUR-PLAY? a) Fighting
HOW RUDE- False (It refers to a man making love to a woman.)

I

I GIVE GREAT FIGARO- c) Join the Paris Opera
I GUESS THEY HAD NO BANANAS- True
I'LL FOLLOW YOU ANYWHERE- False (It's the calf and ankle.)
I LOVE EWE- b) Forced to pay a tax
I'M STUMPED- a) An amputee
IN A PICKLE- c) Homosexuality
INCHING ALONG- True
INCH WORM- True
IN LIKE FLYNN- All three (a,b & c)
INSIDE INFORMATION- False (They are dried bulls' penises.)
IN THE STARS- False (By nibbling their neck.)
I TOAD YOU SO- True
IT PAYS TO ADVERTISE- a) Scratching with their middle finger
IT'S A BALL- True
IT'S A RAP- c) Terrified resistance
I'VE BEEN SLIMED!- True
I'VE GOT A SECRETION- c) Musth

J

JACK THE ZIPPER- False (He was referring to Frank Sinatra.)
JUNEAU THAT?- True

K

KEEP THE TIP- False (They poked it with a stick.)
KLIS ME GOODBYE- b) An enema
KNOT FUNNY- False (They tie a heavy weight to the end.)

L

LADIES AND GENITALMEN- True
LADY BYRD SINGS THE BLUES- False (It was JFK.)
LAID TO REST- True
LAWN JOCKEY- False (You do it for money.)
LETTER PERFECT- b) Doesn't enjoy sex
LIP SERVICE- False (It read, "No Kissing Zone.")
LISTEN UP- False (You were performing oral sex.)
LITTLE BUGGER- a) Stabs it through her back

LITTLE DEVILS- False (They thought they were parasites.)
LOCK-HER ROOM- True
LOOK ON THE BRIGHT SIDE- b) Gout
LOTUS ENTERTAIN YOU- True
LOVE THAT TIE- True
LOWE LIFE- True
LOWER PLEASE- True
LUG NUTS- False (It's the Japanese Dolphin.)

M

MAKE MINE PISTACHIO-True
MAKING A LONG STORY SHORT- False (*Jack & the Beanstalk*)
MAKING A PROPHET- b) Hair of the feet
MASTER STROKE- c) Woody Allen
MAYBE IT'S ANEMIA- True
MEASURING TOOL- False (13 inches)
MERRY QUEEN OF SCOTS- False (It was a term for female genitals.)
MIND OF ITS OWN- True
MIND OVER MAMMARIES- True
MISSION CONTROL- False (They were to insert half a pomegranate.)
MOBY'S DICK- b) Upholster the bar stools on his yacht
MODEL BEHAVIOR- False (He was supposedly bi-sexual.)
MONKEY BUSINESS- False (It has sharp, backward pointing barbs.)
MONKEYING AROUND- b) Urinate in each other's face
MORE CLOVES- True
MOUTHING OFF- b) Illinois
MR. COFFEE- True
MR. RUBBER- c) Colonel Condom
MUSEUM PIECE- a) John Dillinger

N

NO HORSING AROUND- c) In a meat freezer
NUNSENSE- a) Beans

O

OAKEY DOKEY- b) Their acorns resembled a penis.
OCTOPUSSY- b) Her nose
OFF THE SHOULDER- False (They were prostitutes.)
OFF WITH HER HEAD- False (He was referring to the Bible.)
OH GOD- True
OH UNCLE MILTY- True
OH SWELL- False (To the size of an orange)
ONE HUMP OR TWO- a) Once every thirty days

OOPS- True
ORGAN-IZED- c) The Potato Finger
OVAR EASY- a) Oophorectomy
OVER-EXPOSURE- a) The shock of the victim

P

PAP TEST- False (It referred to a homosexual.)
PEE-NALIZED- False (They could only do it if their wives were
immediately available for intercourse.)
PEEPING TOM- True
PENILE INSTITUTION- b) The Great Toe of Corso
PERFECT SCORE- b) 40%
PETER PRINCIPLE- c) Elderly clergy
PICK A WINNER- True
PICTURE THIS- b) "Midnight Cowboy"
PIG IN A POKE- False (It's similar to a corkscrew.)
PORKIN' BEANS- False (He was touching his own testicles.)
POUNDING THE PELTS- False (They go on for hours.)
PRETTY IN PINK- False (It was Jayne Mansfield.)
PRIME CUT- True
PRISON IS NO BALL- True
PUBIC ENEMY- c) Being seen naked
PUPPY CHOW- True
PUSS 'N BOOTS- a) Adolf Hitler
PUT WHAT, WHERE?- c) Dr. Kinsey

Q

QUITE A STRETCH- b) 2 in 1000.

R

RABBIT'S FOOT- False (He urinates on her.)
REAL HOOFER- False (They do it with their eyes closed.)
REDHEAD- c) Long piece of thread
ROCKS OF AGES- False (It meant "apples.")
ROSEY PALM- False (He is dreaming about female genitalia.)
RUB A DUB DUB- c) Scalp
RUNNING MATE- True

S

SAFE BET- False (It's Iowa.)
SAFE SEX- b) Burning wormwood leaves in their navel
SALAMATERNITY- a) Years
SAY AHHH- False (It's your inner nose.)

SAY WHAT?- True

SEE YOU IN SEPTEMBER- True

SHARE AND SHARE ALIKE- False (She had to shave her crotch first.)

SHARK ATTACK- True

SHELL GAME- a) Turns inside out

SHORT HAND- False (You tend to be sexually aggressive.)

SHORT MEMORY- c) Joan Rivers

SHORT STORY- False (It was with George Hamilton.)

SIEG HEIL- True

SIGN IN PLEASE- False (You are most likely a lazy lover.)

SKIN MAGAZINE- True

SLEEPING BEAUTY- c) Fondling a sleeping stranger

SMALL PROBLEM- False (He would have a quiet disposition.)

SMOKIN'- b) Give a woman an orgasm

SNAKE EYES- False (They wrap it in calico.)

SNAP, CRACKLE, POPLESS- b) Tennessee Williams

SO SIOUX ME- a) A buck well spent on a Springmaid sheet

SOUNDS FISHY TO ME- False (They created bi-sexual trout.)

STAND AT ATTENTION- c) Chickens

STRIP SEARCH- a) Search for a flea

SURPRISE- False (He used them as toilet paper holders.)

SWAPPING SEBUM- a) Kissing

T

TALK ABOUT FRIGIDITY- True

TALKING TRASH- True

TENDER MOMENTS- True

THAT'S A LOTTA BULL- True

THE BARD- c) Charged chambers

THE CURE-ALL- False (To eat the heart of a male partridge)

THE EMPEROR HAS NO- False (It was only 1" long.)

THE FRENCH DISCONNECTION- True

THE HARD WAY- True

THE LITTLE RASCALS- False (It was a term for a eunuch.)

THE NATIONAL PASTIME- True

THE RIGHT ANGLE- True

THE TIME OF YOUR LIFE- b) 9 hours

THE YOLK'S ON ME- False (She may be dreaming about disliking sex.)

THEY'RE OFF- b) Guardian of the bed

THREE'S COMPANY- False (You are dreaming about the penis.)

TICKED OFF- b) Nose

TICKLE TICKLE- c) A penis
TIME FOR A RAISE- False (Their best friend of the opposite sex.)
'TIS BETTER TO GIVE- a) The foreskins of 100 Philistines
'TIS THE SEASON- False (It's late summer, early fall.)
TO BEE OR NOT TO BEE- True
TOE THE LINE- True
TOUCHY SITUATION- c) The sole of the foot
TWISTED SISTER- a) 84
TWO FOR THE PRICE OF ONE- True

UNLAWFUL ENTRY- b) Castration
UP ALL NIGHT- a) His lifelong virginity

VIII IS ENOUGH- False (He had illegitimate children.)
VILE CONTENTS- b) Plastic straws

WAIT UP- c) 2 years
WAS IT GOOD FOR YOU?- True
WEIGHT UP- True
WELL HUNG- True
WHAT A BOAR- True
WHATEVER HAPPENED TO GOING BLIND?- False (Blisters on the
                                          nose)
WHAT'S YOUR SIGN- b) Body piercing
WHEN HAIRY MET ARI- b) Bare
WHEN IN FRANCE- b) Kissed someone other than her husband
WHIPPED CREAM- False (Gently scratch the back)
WHITE OUT- True
WHO LEFT THE SEAT UP?- False (By peeping)
WHORE-MONAL THERAPY- b) The vagina is too slippery.
WORN OUT- c) Asparagus

Y

YESSIR ARABFAT- True
YOU'D BE BLUE TOO- b) 110 pounds
YOU PLAY, YOU PAY- c) Lecherwite
YOUR PART'S BEEN CUT- False (Rings were inserted in their
                             foreskins.)

ABOUT THE AUTHORS

Larry Balsamo and Sandra Bergeson have been a successful writing team for over 15 years. They have written everything from trade paperbacks and comedy albums to singing telegrams. "We'll write anything for money," they're both fond of saying.

Although they sometimes bill themselves as, "the nation's most obscure successful writing team," their greatest fame has come in the field of board games. Their collection of 26 somewhat diverse game titles, ranging from **The Couch Potato Game** *and* **Reminiscing** *to "adult" hits like* **Dirty Minds** *and* **Adultrivia***, have sold millions of copies throughout the U.S. and five other countries.*

After ten years of being told at cocktail parties," Hey, those games of yours would make great books," they finally listened and developed **Conversation Books.** *Like many of their board games, the book series is designed to entertain groups through social interaction.*

Larry and Sandy both live in suburban Chicago where, using their eclectic backgrounds in music, magic, opera, stage performance and hucksterism, they founded TDC Games, Inc., a ten year old company they often refer to as, "One of the world's smallest multi-national corporations."

Other Conversation Books

The Book of Indecent Proposals

What would you do for money...lots of money? This book proposes hundreds of provocative tasks. Everyone must reveal if they would perform them in exchange for serious cash. The real fun is trying to predict what others will do for their "dirty money." (Item #5030)

Family, The Book That's Not For Strangers

This is the first book for close relatives, about close relatives. Hundreds of questions are posed that only close family members could answer about each other. Guaranteed to rock the family boat with laughter. (Item #5040)

Harassment, The Book That Let's You Be the Judge

One of the most controversial subjects of our time is addressed with over 150 thought provoking case histories, along with arguments both pro and con. Play judge or predict what others would consider harassment. Then be prepared to defend yourself. (Item#5020)

TO ORDER THESE OR ANY TDC PRODUCT, CALL TOLL FREE 1-800-292-7676.